Anonymous

The Right of the Eldest Sons of the Peers of Scotland

Anonymous

The Right of the Eldest Sons of the Peers of Scotland

ISBN/EAN: 9783337155254

Printed in Europe, USA, Canada, Australia, Japan

Cover: Foto ©Suzi / pixelio.de

More available books at **www.hansebooks.com**

THE

RIGHT

OF THE

ELDEST SONS

OF THE

PEERS of SCOTLAND

TO REPRESENT THE

COMMONS of that Part of GREAT BRITAIN in PARLIAMENT,

CONSIDERED.

PRINTED IN THE YEAR MDCCXC.

T H E

R I G H T

O F   T H E

Eldeſt Sons of the Peers of Scotland,

&c. &c. &c.

C O N S I D E R E D.

———————————

THE Houſe of Commons having lately declared a Seat vacant, in conſequence of a Rule, ſuppoſed to have obtained in Scotland, before the Union, that the eldeſt Son of a Peer is incapable of repreſenting the Commons in Parliament, thoſe immediately intereſted were led to conſider, Whether there really was ſuch a Rule of Law, and upon what Foundation a Notion ſo ſingular could reſt? A noble Lord * favoured the Public with his Thoughts on the Subject, dictated by a Regard to his Order, and a Spirit of free Inquiry, which does him honour. Since that Publication, much Light has been afforded by the Reſearches and Obſervations of another noble Lord †; and their Labours make it an eaſy Taſk to ſtate the Merits of the Queſtion clearly and conciſely, for the Information of thoſe who have not Leiſure or Inclination to peruſe the Argument and Authorities at large.

* Lord Saltoun.   † Lord Daer.

It

It may be remarked in the Outſet, that thoſe who are moſt concerned in the Queſtion profeſs to aim, not at the *Acquiſition*, but at the *Recovery*, of a Privilege : not to *alter* a Part of the Conſtitution, but to *reſtore* it. There is a wide Difference between recurring to theoretical Principles, and aſſerting a conſtitutional Right once acknowledged, and aboliſhed by no Law, the Exerciſe of which is alleged to be ſuſpended only, either from thoſe entitled not claiming it, or from the erroneous Deciſions of Judges. The Right of electing to Parliament cannot be loſt by diſuſe. There are many Inſtances in England of Places, which had neglected to ſend Repreſentatives for Centuries, being reſtored to the Franchiſe, whenever it was claimed. Much leſs can the Capability of being elected be loſt, for that is the Birth-right of every Subject not excluded by poſitive Law. The Hiſtory of Scotland ſhows that the whole Body of Landholders, other than the Nobility, had neglected to attend Parliament, for ſo long a Time, that their Right came to be doubted ; but it was recognized as ſoon as the ancient Practice was aſcertained. In later Times, there is an Inſtance of a County in that Kingdom being reſtored to the Right of ſending Repreſentatives after long diſuſe.

1560.

A Deciſion of the proper Judicature, That a Perſon is incapable of being elected, though it binds the particular Caſe, and the Parties, irrevocably, cannot alter the Law, even when it profeſſes to lay down a general Rule. If the Exiſtence of the Right is proved in a ſubſequent Caſe, no liberal Man will oppoſe the Reſumption of it ; and if the Error of former Determinations is demonſtrated, Judges are bound to reverſe the Principle.

Upon theſe Grounds, the Claim of the Eldeſt Sons of the Peers of Scotland ſhall here be conſidered. It is not meant to introduce Arguments from Expediency ; to aſk, Whether it is reaſonable to exclude for a Time, from the Legiſlative Body, Men, who, by their Birth, muſt one Day make a Part of it ? to exclude them at a Time of Life when they can be moſt uſeful, becauſe they *may be* included at an after

2   uncertain

uncertain Period? or, Whether a Diftinction ought to be made between the Sons of Englifh and of Scots Peers, whilft Mr. Hatfell's
Pofition is indifputable, that, " It is of great Importance that young
" Noblemen fhould pafs through the Houfe of Commons to the Houfe
" of Lords, as a School in which they hear the firft Principles of the
" Conftitution ably and freely debated, and where they acquire Ideas
" of Freedom and Independence, and contract Habits of Bufinefs ?"

Precedents,
Vol. ii. p.
13.

That the eldeft Son of a Peer of Scotland is incapable of being elected
to reprefent a County or a Borough in that Part of Great Britain, is a
Propofition for which no *written* Authority can be produced, except
two Refolutions of the Parliament of Scotland; one in 1685, and another in 1689, and a Refolution of the Britifh Houfe of Commons in
1708. There is not a Word in the Statute Book to give Countenance
to it. There is not a Syllable to that Purpofe in any Writer upon the
Law of Scotland before the Union.

Though there is reafon to think, the firft of thofe Refolutions in the
Scots Parliament paffed without Obfervation or Confideration, and the
fecond with very little; though both appear to have originated in
Party; and though the Refolution of the Britifh Houfe of Commons
feems to have had no Foundation but the Scots ones; it may readily
be admitted, that the Refolutions are entitled to Refpect, efpecially
after the laft has been fo long feemingly acquiefced in; that they are
prima facie Evidence of the Law; and that it lies upon thofe who
impugn them, and the Evidence they afford, to fhow in the moft fatif-
factory Manner that they were erroneous. If that can be done, it will
not be faid that Error fhould be perfifted in. It will not be contended
by any Perfon acquainted with legal Principles, that thofe Refolutions
have the Force of general Laws, and much lefs that general Law could
in that Shape be abrogated.

This is what the eldeft Sons of the Peers of Scotland muft under-
take to do. And as the Refolutions, though not fupported by written
Law, may be fuppofed to have been founded in unwritten Law or
Cuftom,

Cuftom, unlefs the contrary is proved, it is neceflary to fhow what the Law and Cuftom of Scotland, in ancient Times, was in this refpect.

It is therefore propofed here ; 1ft, To fhew, that by the Conftitution of the Parliament of Scotland, prior to the Year 1587, when the Reprefentation of the Counties was eftablifhed, the eldeft Sons of Peers, when poffeffed of Qualifications, muft *of neceffity* have been, and in fact were, conftituent Members. 2dly, To confider, whether the Act paffed in 1587, which difpenfed with the Attendance of the Landholders under the Degree of Peers, and required that they fhould appear thereafter, by their Reprefentatives, or any fubfequent Statute, excluded the eldeft Sons of Peers from choofing, or being themfelves chofen, parliamentary Reprefentatives of the Landholders. 3dly, To give an Account of the Refolutions and other Tranfactions in Parliament fince the Year 1587, which are fuppofed to affect the Right of the Peers eldeft Sons ; and make fome Obfervations upon them. And, laftly, To confider the Arguments ufed by Writers and others, who contend for the Exclufion, or fuppofe it a Point fettled.

Conftitution of the Scots Parliament prior to 1587.

I. The Parliament of Scotland differed in its Conftitution and Form of Proceedings from the Parliament of England in feveral Particulars. From the earlieft Period, down to the Time of the Union, the Lords and Commons formed but one Houfe, and voted promifcuoufly. The Parliament confifted, however, of three diftinct Bodies or *Eftates*, which were a Check on one another, in fome Points, unneceffary to be here mentioned. The firft *Eftate* was that of the Clergy, compofed of the Prelates and other Dignitaries. The fecond was compofed of all the Landholders, Tenants of the King *in capite*, whether Lords or Commons, and whether their Eftates were great or fmall, under the Denomination of Barons or Freeholders ; for the Term *Freeholder* is in Scotland applied only to thofe who hold Lands of the Crown. The Reprefentatives of the Royal Burghs made the third Eftate. At what Period they were introduced into Parliament is not known ; but, comparatively with the Barons, it was at a late one.

Parliament

Parliament was originally no other than an Aſſembly of the King's Vaſſals in his Court, as paramount Lord, or Superior, of all the Lands in the Country. The Attendance was an Obligation, neceſſarily ariſing from their Tenure, in the ſame way as the Vaſſals of Meſne Lords, or Subject Superiors, were bound to give Suit and Preſence in their Courts. Hence, none but the *immediate* Vaſſals of the Crown were admitted, or, more properly ſpeaking, were *compellable to attend* Parliament, and all who held immediately of the Crown were conſtituent Members. Hence, likewiſe, the Introduction of the Repreſentatives of Royal Burghs. The Burgeſſes held their Lands and Tenements ſeverally of the King, and every one of them was entitled, as his Tenant, to a Seat in Parliament; but, that being inconvenient, they were allowed to attend by their Repreſentatives. Lord Stair, treating of the Feudal Syſtem, writes thus: " In Scotland the King, " as ſupreme Superior, ruleth *by his Vaſſals aſſembled in Parliament*, in " which, at firſt, all were perſonally preſent, who held Lands im- " mediately of him; as Barons, great and ſmall Freeholders of any " Moment, holding a Forty Shilling Land, of old Extent, of the " King, and Prelates for Church Lands. The free Burghs were alſo " repreſented in Parliament by their Commiſſioners, as holding " Burgage Lands, and their Freedoms and Privileges, as Feudatories " of the King: ſo that there was not one Foot of Ground in Scotland " whoſe Lord was not preſent in Parliament, by himſelf or his De- " legate. But when Feus holden of the King came to be ſubdivided " and multiplied, two or more Commiſſioners were admitted in Par- " liament, in Name of the meaner Barons or Freeholders." To the ſame Purpoſe, Lord Bankton: " Originally with us, *none had a Seat in Par-* " *liament but thoſe poſſeſſed of a Freehold of the King.* Thus the Biſhops, " and likewiſe the Peers, ſat in reſpect of their Baronies, all Nobility " and Peerage being of old territorial; and the other Freeholders were " all entitled to ſit in Parliament, *and bound to attend*, till the Small " Barons,

Lord Kaims's Eſſays on Britiſh Antiquities, and other Authorities.

Lord Stair's Inſtitutions, B. 2. Tit. 3.

Lord Bankton's Inſtitute, B. 4. Tit. 1. § 8.

" Barons, *as a Privilege*, were exempted, and allowed to choose Com-
" missioners to represent them."

The three *Estates* of Parliament. continued as above mentioned till the
Revolution, when the Estate of the Clergy being annihilated, and it
being reckoned necessary, as it would seem, still to have the Name of
three Estates, the Nobility were separated from the other Landholders,
and made the first Estate. The Representatives of those other Landholders, or Lesser Barons, as they were called (for Representation in
Counties had some Time before taken place, as shall be afterwards
mentioned), made the second Estate. And the Burgh Representatives
continued to be the third.

Hereditary Titles of Nobility were conferred by the King, in Scotland,
from the most ancient Times of which any Record remains. It is
certain that these Peerages were anciently territorial, and passed with the
Land ; as the Authorities quoted above, and many others which might
be referred to, shew. They were afterwards personal, conferred by
Patent, or by Investiture in Parliament. Those who held such Honours,
came to be called *Noblemen, Lords of Parliament,* and *Greater Barons,*
to distinguish them from the Freeholders, or *Lesser Barons,* but still
they continued of the same *Estate,* with the general Body of the Freeholders or Barons ; nor is there any Reason or Authority for thinking,
that, *in Parliament,* they enjoyed any Privilege beyond the Lesser Barons,
except that of Rank and Precedency. It may be supposed, that after
Peerages came to be conferred without Regard to any particular Territory, the Holders were considered as constituent Members of Parliament, and that they sat *as Peers,* rather than *as the King's Vassals* ; though
it is scarcely to be imagined, that there ever was one of them without
Lands held of the King, and consequently not entitled to attend
Parliament, and to be of the same *Estate* as a Freeholder, independent
of his Peerage. The *Obligation* might thus in Idea be changed into a
Privilege, analogous to the hereditary Counsellorship annexed to the

Peerage

Case of Lady
Sutherland,
by Lord
Hailles,
chap. 4.

Peerage in England. But, however that may be, the Eftate of the Barons, including both the Greater and Smaller, was ftill confidered as *repre-fenting the Land of the Kingdom*, and they were all, fo far as is known, upon the fame Footing, when met.

It is proved indifputably, by the Records, that before the Introduction of Reprefentatives for the Counties, eldeft Sons of the Peers or Nobles attended Parliament, and were accounted as belonging to the Eftate of Barons or Landholders, Tenants of the King *in cafite*. Upon this, the prefent Queftion mainly hinges; and it is therefore hoped, that thofe who wifh to form a fair Judgment upon it, will attend to the Fact, and the neceffary Inferences from it.

That there fhould not be many Inftances of the eldeft Sons of Peers attending as conftituent Members, is not wonderful; becaufe none but thofe who held *freehold* Lands in their own Right, could attend, or were admiffible. One Inftance, well authenticated, would afford Evidence of what is meant to be eftablifhed, as good as a thoufand. But there are many, and in fuch various Situations, as ferve to refute all the Suppofitions of thofe who, forced to admit the Fact, endeavour to explain it, in Confiftency with the Hypothefis of the Peers Sons not being *efficient* Members.

There are no authentic Rolls of the Members who attended Parliament till the Year 1466, in the Reign of James III. but from that Time, the Records are exifting in tolerable Prefervation, down to the Union in 1707. At the opening of each Parliament, or Seffion, there is generally a Roll containing the Names of the Members then prefent, or, in the later Times, containing the Names alfo of all who appear to have attended on future Days, during the Seffion.

See Copies of the Rolls, in the Appendix.

A Search of the Records has afforded the Names of above thirty eldeft Sons of Peers in Parliament, moft of them fitting in two or three different Parliaments; fo that, on the whole, there are Inftances, to the Number of fifty-feven or thereby, of their being prefent. The firft, is on the 1ft of March 1478-9, and the laft, on the 29th of

B

November

November 1558; after which, none are mentioned in the Rolls preserved in the public Register: but besides thefe, there is a Lift of the Members of the Parliament or Convention in 1560, well authenticated; by which it appears, that feveral of the eldeft Sons of Peers then attended. That the eldeft Sons did not attend as Proxies for their Fathers, as has been ignorantly alleged, is proved by the Fathers fitting at the fame Time, in twenty-four Inftances; and that they fat and acted as conftituent or efficient Members, is demonftrated by the Circumftance of their being appointed on Committees; there is an Inftance particularly of the Earl of Huntley's eldeft Son being of the Committee of Articles, the Importance of which every one, who is the leaft converfant in Scots Hiftory, knows, and. that, while his Father was alfo attending Parliament.

There is no Reafon for fuppofing, that the Peers Sons, who are thus proved to have attended, fat in any other Character than that of Leffer Barons, or Freeholders, entitled by their private Properties. Lord Kaims, in his Effay on the Conftitution of Parliament, fays, " In later Times (meaning not long before 1587), the Barons by " Tenure, who attended Parliament, were moftly the eldeft Sons of " the Nobility *infeft in* (i. e. feifed of) *Lands, to entitle them to a* " *Seat there.*" It is not eafy, at this Diftance of Time, confidering the Change of Property, and the Imperfection of the Regifter of Charters and *Seafins*, to afcertain what precife Lands were enjoyed by the Peers eldeft Sons who are marked as fitting in Parliament; but in fundry Inftances it can be proved by the Records, that they actually had, in their own Right, Eftates entitling them to fit as Leffer Barons. According to feudal Principles, if the eldeft Son of a Peer, poffeffed Lands held of the King, he muft of *Neceffity* have attended Parliament or forfeited his Eftate; unlefs recourfe is had to fo wild a Suppofition, as that the King in every fuch Cafe difpenfed with the Attendance; and therefore, though the Records had not afforded a fingle Inftance of a Perfon, in that Situation, attending, the only Inference would. have been, that no eldeft Son of a Peer had happened

In the Cottonian Library.

Kaims's Effays, p. 99.

to

to be poffeffed of freehold Lands ; but the Right in Law would have been the fame. If the eldeft Son of a Peer fucceeded to a Dignity, or Greater Barony, by the maternal Line, or by collateral Succeffion, it will not be contended, furely, that he was incapable of fitting in Parliament, by virtue of that Title, though at the fame Time apparent Heir of his Father's Dignity ; and, by Parity of Reafon, and in precife Conformity with the Conftitution, if he fucceeded to a *Leffer* Barony, or acquired one during his Father's life, he muft have been inftantly intitled to a Seat as a Leffer Baron.

The Conclufion from all this, may be laid down with perfect Confidence, *That, prior to the Year* 1587, *the eldeft Sons of Peers were admiffible to Parliament, like other Landholders, and when there were of that Eftate or Clafs which correfponds to the Reprefentatives of the Commons, in modern Times.*

II. The next Thing to be confidered, is, the Alteration made in the Conftitution of Parliament, by allowing Reprefentatives for the *Leffer Barons*, inftead of compelling their perfonal Attendance ; and Whether the eldeft Sons of Peers who happened to be Leffer Barons, poffeffed of Freeholds in their own Right, and who had previoufly been entitled to fit in Parliament, were excluded from having a Voice in the Election of thofe Reprefentatives, or from being themfelves chofen.

Alteration in the Conftitution of the Scots Parliament.

It has been mentioned, that attending Parliament was a feudal Obligation or Burden acceffary to the Tenure. The Burden was, of courfe, moft felt by thofe who had fmall Poffeffions, and their Number, by the fplitting of Property, was continually increafing. By an Act of James I. in 1425, the perfonal Attendance of all Freeholders, without Diftinction, was ftrictly required. It is probable that this was complained of as a Grievance ; becaufe, within two Years after (1427), another Act was paffed, difpenfing with the Attendance of the *fmall Barons and free Tenants*, provided they fent two Reprefentatives or Commiffioners from each Sheriffdom. It was thus left optional to attend in Perfon or by Reprefentation.   The Term, *Small Barons*, in this Act, is ufed in

the

the literal Senfe, fignifying thofe who had fmall Properties, and not, as it came afterwards to be ufed, in Contradiftinction to the Greater Barons or Peers. Accordingly, by fubfequent Statutes, in the Reigns of James II. and IV. the Extent of the Property which intitled the Holder to Difpenfation from perfonal Attendance, and to choofe Reprefentatives, is precifely afcertained. During the Period from 1427 to 1587, the *Eftate* of the Barons in Parliament might have been diftinguifhed into three Claffes. 1ft, The Greater, or Nobility. 2d, The Barons, or Freeholders, under the Degree of Nobility, but poffeffed of Eftates of too high a Value to be permitted to fit by Reprefentatives. And 3d, The Reprefentatives of the Small Barons. But, in fact, the Privilege given by the Acts prior to 1587, was never exercifed. The Barons Eftate in Parliament was compofed as formerly of the Peers, and Barons under the Degree of Peers, who chofe to attend, including the eldeft Sons of Peers who happened to be poffeffed of freehold Lands, in their own Right. By the Roll of the Convention Parliament, held in 1560, there appear to have attended, 28 of the Clergy ; 33 of the Nobility, amongft whom are particularly to be remarked, the Earls of Marifhall and Glencairn, and the Lords Sommerville and Lindefay ; 101 Leffer Barons, amongft whom are five eldeft Sons of Peers, the *Mafters* of Marifhall, Glencairn, Sommerville, Lindefay, and Sinclair ; and 22 Commiffioners or Reprefentatives of Burghs. The eldeft Sons of Peers, at that Period, were diftinguifhed by their Father's Title, with the Addition of *Mafter*. Thus, Lord Marifhall's eldeft Son was ftyled, *The Mafter of Marifhall*. His fecond Son would have been called Mr. Keith.

James VI.
Parliament
II. C.114.

In the Year 1587, an Act was paffed which deferves particular Attention. It recites the Act of James I. 1427, ratifies it, and directs, that it fhould be carried into Execution in Time coming. And it enacts, That *Commiffioners to Parliament* fhould thereafter be elected for each County, and that *all Freeholders of the King, under the Degree of Prelates and Lords of Parliament*, fhould be warned by Proclamation to be prefent at the choofing of the Commiffioners, and thofe who had

3

a forty

a forty Shilling Land in free Tenantry, holden of the King, fhould
have Voices in the Election. The Act concludes with a Declaration,
" That the Appearance of the faid Commiffioners of the Shires in Par-
" liaments and general Councils, fhould *relieve* the Whole other Small
" Barons and Freeholders of the Shire of their Suits and Prefence in
" Parliament."

Though this Act does not exprefsly difcharge the Barons and Freeholders, under the Degree of Prelates, and Lords of Parliament, from
perfonal Attendance, yet it was fo underftood. What has been re-
peatedly mentioned, That the Attendance was confidered as a Burden,
not as a Privilege, is a Key to this, as well as other Things. They were
to be *relieved* from Suit and Prefence, if they fent Commiffioners; and,
as it was not to be fuppofed that any would reject that proffered Relief,
the Claufe was tantamount to exprefsly debarring perfonal Attendance.

Accordingly, from the Time of paffing this Act, none of the Leffer
Barons appear to have fat in Parliament but as Reprefentatives by
Election, and Reprefentatives were regularly chofen for the Counties.

From this Period, the Term Smaller or *Leffer Barons* was applied
ftrictly to all Freeholders under the Degree of Lords of Parliament,
holding Lands of the Extent mentioned in the Act, and the Term
Greater Barons diftinguifhed the Peers. But ftill the Greater Barons,
and the Reprefentatives of the Leffer, made only *one Eftate* in Parliament.

From this Period too, it is admitted, that the Name of no eldeft Son
of a Peer is to be found in the Rolls of Parliament that are extant, nor
is there any other Evidence that they fat, or attempted to fit, till the
End of the following Century. From hence, it has been argued, That
this Act of 1587 *muft have been underftood* to exclude them from
a Voice in the Election of the Reprefentatives of the Leffer
Barons, and from being themfelves elected. So the Argument, if
it deferves the Name, muft be ftated; for it cannot be pretended,
that the Act contains one Word, which can be wrefted into any Thing
like a direct Exclufion, or one Expreffion which can with any Propriety
be faid to be aimed at the Peers Sons in particular. The only Colour
which

which the Argument derives from the Act, is the Coincidence of its Date, and of the eldeft Sons of Peers ceafing to appear in Parliament. Even this might be difputed ; for, in fact, they had ceafed attending, if their Non-appearance in the Rolls can be called fo, thirty Years before; and there are no Rolls extant for 27 Years after, in which Period there were frequent Parliaments: fo that, for ought that is known, the eldeft Sons of Peers may have been elected, and have fat as entitled by the Terms of the Act 1587.

The eldeft Sons of the Peers have no Occafion to prevent their Oppo-nents from making any Ufe they pleafe of this Act, and of every other in the Statute Book. In return, they may found upon it, as decifive of the Queftion in their favour.

It feems a fair Argument, That, whether the eldeft Sons of Peers fat in Parliament before this Time or not, yet, under the general compre-henfive Words of the Act 1587, which grants the Privilege of electing, and confequently of being elected Commiffioners, *to all Freeholders of the King under the Degree of Prelates and Lords of Parliament*, the eldeft Sons of Peers, having Freeholds, are included, becaufe it is impoffible to maintain that they were at the paffing of this Act, called or underftood to be *Lords of Parliament.* It might as well be faid, that they were *Prelates. Lord of Parliament* is a Term of Defcription fynonymous with Greater Baron, in contradiftinction to Leffer Baron, or a Perfon of inferior Order, and correfponds almoft exactly to the Englifh Term, *Peer of Par-liament.* In Scotland, when a Perfon of an inferior Order was to be made a Noble of the loweft Clafs, it was not done by creating him a Baron, or granting him a Barony, as in England ; but it was, by creat-ing him *a Lord of Parliament*, either by Patent, or by Inveftiture. *Baron*, in the legal Senfe of the Term, in Scotland, is a Perfon, whether Noble or Commoner, who holds Lands with certain Privileges ; as the Territory, to the holding of which thefe Privileges are annexed, is called *the Barony.* In parliamentary Language, *Baron* is a Perfon who holds Lands in any way of the King, and the fame as *Freeholder.*

By

By the Words, *Under the Degree of Lords of Parliament*, in the Act 1587, is meant under *the Rank of Nobility;* and therefore, even suppofing it had not been fhewn that the eldeft Sons of Peers fat in Parliament prior to the Act 1587, as Leffer Barons, by virtue of their Freeholds; or that it could be fhewn that they never did ; ftill the fair and legal Conclufion, from the Terms of the Act, would be, that the Privilege of electing, and being elected,. Reprefentatives of the Leffer Barons, was meant *to be conferred* on them, when poffeffed of Freeholds, there not being a Syllable in the Act to exclude them.

But without carrying the Argument that Length, and taking the Act in. the Senfe in which it has been generally underftood, namely, as intended to draw a line of Diftinction between the Peers, or Greater Barons, and the Commoners, or Leffer Barons, leaving the *former* precifely in the fame Situation they were ; that is, conftituent Members of Parliament, whofe perfonal Attendance was required ;. and excluding the great Body of the *latter*, fo that, from that Time forward, they fhouldhave a Right to fit only by their Reprefentatives ; the Act, when coupled with the indifputable Fact of the Peers eldeft Sons having been previoufly admitted, and conftantly in ufe, to fit as Leffer Barons, when they had that Character in them, is decifive, and what they found upon it may be ftated in the Shape of a Syllogifm.

By the Act of 1587, all Perfons then belonging to the *Eftate* of Barons, under the Degree of Prelates and Lords of Parliamént, were excluded from perfonal Attendance ; and, in lieu of it, a Privilege was conferred upon them of electing, and of being elected, Reprefentatives of the Leffer Barons.

The eldeft Sons of Peers, being under the Degree of Prelates, and Lords of Parliament, were of the Eftate of Barons, and fat in Parliament when poffeffed of Freeholds, and confequently were of the Number excluded by the Act from attending perfonally.

Therefore by the Act, they became, and are, entitled to elect, or to be elected, Reprefentatives.

This

This Act of 1587 is still in force; and is the Basis of all the Election Laws for Scotland.

The only other Statutes respecting Elections, before the Union, are those of Charles II. Parliament I. 1661. C. 35. and Parliament III. 1681. C. 21. By these, the Estates and Qualifications of the Electors are defined, more precisely than they were by the Act of 1587; and Residence in the County, which that Act required, in the elected, is dispensed with; but the Right of electing, and to be elected, is left, as before, open to all Men possessed of the Qualification in Freehold Land, *excepting Noblemen and their Vassals.* As a particular Exception serves to strengthen a general Rule, it seems impossible to dispute, That the Right of electing, and being elected, was given to the eldest Sons of Peers, being Freeholders; or, at least, impossible to contend, That if they had the Right formerly, it was now taken away; unless it can be maintained that they were meant to be described by the Term *Noblemen*, a Term, which in common Language is scarcely ever, and never with Propriety, applied to them, and which certainly was not, nor could be, meant, as a legal Description of them. It was introduced into the Act with Propriety, and stands there as descriptive of the Peers, or Greater Barons, to controul the broad words *all Heritors* (that is, Landholders), which otherwise would have conferred on the Peers a Right to interfere in the Election of the Commons. It is farther to be observed, That the Preamble of the Act 1661 bears, that it was made *to remove all Doubts, as to who were capable of electing or being elected Representatives.* It then declares the Right to be vested in *all Heritors* possessed of Estates, to the Extent therein mentioned, excepting Noblemen and their Vassals. A more safe and unequivocal Authority upon the Point now under consideration cannot be figured.

Resolutions and Entries in the Journals of Parliament, re-

III. So stood the Law and the Practice, with respect to the eldest Sons of Peers, when the following Entry was made in the Minutes or Journals of the Scots Parliament: " Edinburgh, the 23d of April,
" 1685,

" 1685, In refpect, the Vifcount of Tarbat's eldeft Son, elected one of
" the Commiffioners for the Shire of Rofs, *by reafon that his Father is*
" *nobilitated*, cannot now reprefent that Shire, Warrant was given to
" the Freeholders of that Shire to meet and elect another Perfon in his
" Place." lative to the Right of Peers eldeft Sons, with Obferva- tions.

Upon this Refolution, or Memorandum, it fhall only be obferved
here, that the Vifcount of Tarbat was Sir George Mackenzie of Tarbat,
a noted Courtier and Favourite of James II. of England, and VII.
of Scotland, who, at the Beginning of his Reign, raifed him to the
Dignity of a Vifcount. Lord Tarbat held the Office of Regifter, and
as fuch, was Clerk of the Parliaments, and kept and framed the Acts
and Minutes. This Entry is made on the firft Day of Meeting; and
the Terms of it are taken notice of in no Writer at the Time, nor is
there any Reafon to fuppofe that it was attended to. A new Election
for Rofsfhire took place, and therefore it muft have been known that
Lord Tarbat's Son had vacated his Seat; but on what Account he
vacated, might be known to nobody, nor had any one Occafion to
inquire. It is undeniable that the Members of the Scots Parliament
were in ufe to furrender their Seats upon the moft frivolous Pretences.
In the County, for which he fat, a plaufible Reafon would occur:
the whole Eftate of the Family, a Part of which made ʼ ·· Qualification of the Vifcount's eldeft Son, was on the Eve ·ʼ ʼeing dif-
joined from that County, as it actually was, within . Weeks after.
All the Hiftorians and Writers agree (and it is particularly ftated by
Sir George Mackenzie of Rofehaugh, in his Obfervations on the Acts
of Parliament), that it was the Object of James VI. and his ᷾ᴄceffors
to diminifh the Influence of the Nobility, and to throw Weight ʼ ᵒ the
Scale of the Commons in Parliament. To introduce a Precedent, for
depriving the eldeft Sons of the Peers of their Right to fit in Parliament, was agreeable to this Syftem; and no Period could be more
favourable for it, than this of 1685, as no Minifter could be more
pliant than Lord Tarbat. The Character of this Parliament, in which

he

Hume's History, 8vo. Vol. viii. p. 237.

he was one of the chief Rulers, is given by a fingle Stroke of Mr. Hume's Pen : " No Courtier, even the moſt proſtitute, could go " farther than they, towards a Reſignation of their Liberties." And one of the Articles of Grievances voted at the Revolution was in theſe Words : " That moſt of the Laws enacted in the Parliament *Anno* 1685, " are impious and intolerable Grievances."

The next, and only other Reſolution of the Scots Parliament, reſpecting this Subject, is entered in the Journals of the Meeting of the Eſtates or Convention Parliament 1689, in the following Words : " Edinburgh, 18th March 1689, The Meeting of the Eſtates having " heard the Report of the Committee for Elections, bearing, that in " the controverted Election for the Borough of Linlithgow, in Favour " of the Lord Livingſton and William Higgins, it is the Opinion of " the Committee, that William Higgins's Commiſſion ought to be pre- " ferred ; *firſt*, in regard of Lord Livingſton's Incapacity to repreſent a " Borough, being the eldeſt Son of a Peer ; *ſecondly*, in reſpect William " Higgins was more legally and formally elected by the Plurality of " Votes of the Burgeſſes, they have approven, and approves, the ſaid " Report, in both the Heads thereof, and interpones their Authority " thereto."

Upon this Caſe, it is to be obſerved, that the Petition of Mr. Higgins is extant ; and though it is drawn with anxiety, and evidently the Work of no mean Counſel, entering at large into the Proceedings and the Legality of the Votes given for Lord Livingſton, yet the Objection of Incapacity is not taken ; a Proof that it did not occur to the Counſel, or was not conſidered as tenable Ground, and that the prior Reſolution, in the Caſe of Lord Tarbat's Son, was not known, or not held to be a legal Precedent. The Incapacity appears to have been a Diſcovery of the Committee ; and we know from the Hiſtorians and An-

Lord Balcarras's Memoirs ; Sir John Dalrymple's ditto.

naliſts of that Period, that Party then ran high, and ſhowed itſelf particularly in the Deciſion of controverted Elections. The Revolutioniſts, or Whigs, had the Majority, and were reſolved to preſerve it, by ſtarting

9   every

every Objection to thofe of the other Side. Lord Livingſton was a
Tory, and actually in arms for King James. Higgins was of an
oppoſite Complexion, and ſoon after a Preſbyterian Clergyman. It
does not appear that any Defence was ſet up for Lord Livingſton ; and
it is certain he was not preſent ; for the next Day there was a Proclamation iſſued, ſtating that he was at the Head of a Body of Men near
Linlithgow, and requiring him to ſurrender. It may be added, that the
Refolution did not paſs in a regular Parliament, but in the Convention
of the Eſtates aſſembled at the Revolution, a Time ill adapted for an
Examination into *leſſer* Matters of Right.

We paſs next to the Period of the Union.

By the 22d Article of that Treaty, it was agreed, That the Number
of Repreſentatives for Scotland, in the Houſe of Commons of the Parliament of Great Britain, ſhould be forty-five ; and that theſe were to
be elected in ſuch Manner as ſhould be ſettled by an Act of the Parliament of Scotland, which Act was declared to be as valid as if it
were a Part of and engroſſed in the Treaty. A Bill was accordingly
brought into the Parliament of Scotland, and at laſt paſſed into a Law,
for ſettling the Manner of electing the ſixteen Peers, and forty-five
Commoners, to repreſent Scotland in the Parliament of Great Britain.
While the Bill was under conſideration, a Motion was made, to inſert
a Clauſe or Declaration, in theſe Words : " That *no Peer,* nor the
" eldeſt Son of any Peer, can be choſen to repreſent either Shire or
" Burgh, in that Part of the United Kingdom, in the Houſe of Com-
" mons." This aroſe from a prevailing Notion, that the Peers not
elected to repreſent the Nobility in the Houſe of Lords of Great Britain meant to claim the Privilege of being elected into the Houſe of
Commons. The Motion occaſioned a great Debate ; and it was
moved, in place of theſe Words, to inſert the following : " Declaring
" always, that none ſhall elect or be elected to repreſent a Shire or Burgh
" in the Parliament of Great Britain, from this part of the United
" Kingdom, except ſuch as are now capable by the Laws of this King-

Act 8th,
4th Seſſion
Q. Anne's
Parliament.

" dom

" dom to elect or be elected as Commissioners for Shires or Burghs to
" the said Parliament." It was put to the Vote, Whether the *first* or
the *second* Clause should be adopted? and the Majority decided for
the second. In the Scots Parliament, this was the constant Mode of
determining between two opposite or different Propositions; and in
this Case, it was agreed, That the Votes should be marked, and a List
of the Members, showing how they severally voted, recorded, and
printed. It appears, by the List, that there voted,

For the *second* Clause,— Officers of State * --	6	
Peers - -	55	
Representatives of Counties	5	
Representatives of Burghs	20	
Total ———		86
For the *first* Clause,—Officers of State -	1	
Peers - -	1	
Representatives of Counties	47	
Representatives of Burghs	23	
Total ———		72
Majority		14

From hence t 's p   u, That the Peers considered the *second*
clause which was ac ured, as not excluding their eldest Sons; and
satisfied with   Point, they appear to have abandoned the original Design   epen, even to themselves, to be elected; and,
2dly   the great Body of the Commons considered it as at least not
sufficient to   clude Peers Sons; and therefore they pressed for the first
Clause, which   vould have done it effectually. The fair Inference from

* A certain Number of the King's Ministers were Members of the Scots Parliament,
by virtue of their Offices.

the

the whole, is, That the eldeſt Sons of Peers were not, in the Opinion of either Party, incapable by the Law, as it then ſtood ; for, if that had been ſuppoſed, the Peers gained nothing by the Alteration propoſed, and their Opponents had not the leaſt Occaſion to ſtruggle againſt its Adoption ; their Purpoſe being equally anſwered by either of the Clauſes. So far from its being reckoned a clear Point, that the Peers Sons were by the Law and Cuſtom of Scotland incapable of repreſenting the Commons in Parliament, it is noticed by the Reporters of the Debates in the Union Parliament, that the prevailing Argument againſt the Clauſe firſt Propoſed, was, " That it had been always allowed in Scotland be- " fore, that the eldeſt Sons of Peers might be elected ;" and that this was not contradicted by the Members of the oppoſite Side.

Defoe's Hiſtory of the Union, 2d Edition, p. 496.

It being thus ſettled by the Treaty, That the Right of electing and being elected into the Houſe of Commons of Great Britain for Scotland, ſhould be governed by the Rules which had obtained in that Kingdom before the Union, there were choſen in the Parliament of Great Britain, ſummoned in 1708, four eldeſt Sons of Scots Peers ; namely, Lord Johnſtone, eldeſt Son of the Marquis of Annandale, for Dumfriesſhire, and alſo for Linlithgowſhire ; Lord Haddo, eldeſt Son of the Earl of Aberdeen, for Aberdeenſhire ; Lord Strathnaver, eldeſt Son of the Earl of Sutherland, for the Borough of Tain, &c. ; and Mr. Sinclair, eldeſt Son of Lord Sinclair, for the Boroughs of Dyſart. &c. Petitions were preſented to the Houſe of Commons, complaining of all theſe Elections. Thoſe againſt Lord Johnſtone, Lord Strathnaver, and Mr. Sinclair, ſtated various Objections, beſides alleging generally, that the ſitting Members were incapable of being elected as the eldeſt Sons of Peers. The Petition againſt Lord Haddo was confined to the ſingle Point of the Incapacity, and went at large into what were no doubt reckoned *the Merits* of the Caſe. It is worth while to ſtate the Argument in the Words of the Petition. After mentioning the Terms of the Treaty of Union, and the Relative Act of the Scots Parliament, it proceeds, " That the eldeſt " Son of any Peer of the Realm could not ſit as a Commiſſioner to re- " preſent

Commons Journals, Nov. 7, 1708.

" prefent any Shire or Borough in the Parliament of Scotland, as is evi-
" dent from the following remarkable Inftances, now extant upon the
" Records of Parliament, viz." [Here the Refolutions of 1685 and
" 1689 are quoted] " That, neverthelefs, the Power and Influence of
" the Scottifh Nobility is fo great, that in many Places their eldeft Sons
" have at this Time been chofen to reprefent both Shires and Burghs in
" the Houfe of Commons of Great Britain, and particularly in the Shire
" of Aberdeen ; which the Petitioners conceive is *(at this Juncture)* a
" Precedent of that confequence, that, if not prevented, the Electors and
" Freeholders in future Time will never be able to withftand fo Power-
" ful an Intereft, but rather, by continual Difcouragements, the Majority
" of them muft become fubfervient to the Nobility, in diftreffing all thofe
" who fhall have the Courage to refift their incroaching upon, or giving
" up, the Rights and Privileges of the Commons : And praying, that the
" Houfe will take the Matter into confideration, not only as it relates to
" a prefent Incroachment made on the Petitioners particular Rights and
" Privileges, but (what is of far greater Moment) as, in all Probability, it
" will, in a very fhort Time, fenfibly affect the very Being and Confti-
" tution of a Britifh Houfe of Commons, by bringing our fmall Repre-
" fentation into the Hands of a numerous and powerful Peerage, the
" Confequence whereof they have but too great Caufe to fear, and fub-
" mit themfelves, Liberties, and Privileges, into the fecure Protection
" and wife Provifion of a Britifh Parliament."

Upon thefe Petitions being prefented, the Houfe of Commons appointed a Day for taking into confideration that Part of the Act for uniting
the two Kingdoms which relates to the Election of Members to ferve for
that Part of Great Britain called Scotland. And it appears by the Journals, that, upon the 3d of December 1708, Counfel were heard, and the
Petitions and Reprefentations relating to that Matter were again read ; and
a Motion being made, and the Queftion put, " That the eldeft Sons of
" the Peers of Scotland were capable, by the Laws of Scotland at the
" Time of the Union, to elect or be elected as Commiffioners for Shires
" or

" or Boroughs to the Parliament of Scotland ; and therefore, by the
" Treaty of Union, are capable to elect or be elected to reprefent any
" Shire or Burgh in Scotland, to fit in the Houfe of Commons of Great
" Britain,"—it paffed in the negative.   On the 6th of December, new
Writs were ordered for Linlithgow and Aberdeenfhire, in the room of
Lord Johnftone and Lord Haddo, " declared to be incapable to fit in the
" Houfe, being the eldeft Sons of Peers of that Part of Great Britain
" called Scotland." The Seats of Lord Strathnaver and Mr. Sinclair were
afterwards vacated in the fame Manner.

No fatisfactory Account remains of what was urged upon this Occafion in the Houfe of Commons. If Chandler's Debates can be trufted
to, the Petitioners offered no Proof of their Affertion that Peers eldeft Sons
were incapable by the Law of Scotland, except the Refolutions of 1685
and 1689 ; and the Advocates on that Side of the Queftion entered
into general Declamation concerning the Danger to the Liberties of the
Commons of Scotland, if the Peers Sons were declared capable, and the
Expediency of diminifhing the Influence of the Peers themfelves, by an
Exclufion of their Heirs Apparent. Chandler fays, " *little was offered*
" *on the other Side.*" It is even uncertain, whether the fitting Members appeared by Counfel. A Hiftorian has mentioned, with the
Appearance of Probability, " That the Peers of Scotland refted in confi- Scot's Hif-
" dence that the Members would not fuffer their eldeft Sons to be fo de- tory of
" graded, fince the eldeft Sons of the Englifh Peers enjcyed the Pri- Scotland, p.
" vilege."   746.

The Refpect which is due to all Determinations of the Houfe of Commons, does not permit one to fay, That the declamatory Arguments which
the Petitions fhow were principally relied on by thofe who attacked the
Right of the fitting Members, could have any Influence, though it is well
known, that in Election Matters, the Houfe *was* lefs chafte than in others.
A Writer, who would have been the laft to affix a Stigma to their Pro- Mr. Hat-
ceedings, if a Regard to Truth and the Conftitution had not extorted it fell's Prece-
                                                                  dents, Vol.
                                              from ii. p. 13.

from him, fays, " Under the *former* Judicature for deciding controverted
" Elections, every Principle of Decency and Juſtice were notorioully
" and openly proſtituted."

In the preſent Caſe it appears, from the Way in which the Motion was
worded, that the Houſe took up the Matter properly, conſidering
themſelves as deciding a Queſtion *of Fact*; namely, What the Law of
Scotland on the Point was before the Union; not what it ought to
have been, or what was the moſt expedient Rule for the Time to come.
It ſeems to be highly probable, that the Facts and the Law in favour
of the Rights of Scots Peers eldeſt Sons, were not fully explained to
the Engliſh Houſe of Commons, who could hardly be Maſters of the
Subject, and who at that critical Moment might be ſuppoſed ready to
yield to any Thing repreſented to be the general Senſe and Inclination
of the Commons in Scotland. If ſuch Proofs had been then brought,
and ſuch Arguments uſed, as the Caſe, when now examined, admits
of, it will hardly be thought too preſumptuous to ſay the Determination would probably have been different. But ſuppoſing the Houſe
of Commons, in 1708, had before them all the Lights which the
Subject required, it is not yet too late to aſk and expect a Reconſider-
ation of it. If the eldeſt Sons of the Peers of Scotland can ſhow that
they were and are eligible by the Law of the Land, their Right cannot be cut off, either by thoſe Reſolutions of the Scots Parliament, in
1685 and 1689, or by that of the Britiſh Houſe of Commons in
1708; for no Man will pretend, that the Reſolutions have in themſelves the Force of Law, much leſs, that they can repeal poſitive Law.
The Reſolutions are, at the beſt, only in execution of what thoſe who
made them underſtood to be the Law; but if they erred, the Error may
and muſt be corrected when diſcovered and demonſtrated. Upon ſuch
Principles, ſanctioned by the Opinion of the Judges, the Houſe of
Lords, in 1782, with a Liberality which does them infinite Honour,
reverſed a Reſolution come to in 1711, whereby the Peers of Scotland
had

had been declared incapable of fitting in that House, by virtue of Patents of British Peerage conferred on them after the Union.

The only hiftorical Facts which remain to be ftated, are, that in two Inftances, viz. That of Lord Charles Douglas, in 1754, and Mr. Charteris, in 1787, the Seats of Scots Members were declared to be vacated, in purfuance of the Rule laid down in 1708, no regular Oppofition being made. And two other Cafes have occurred, which deferve to be noticed: 1ft, The eldeft Son of the Duke of Atholl having ¹ Geo. I. been attainted, the Honours of that Family were, by Act of Parliament, vefted in Lord James Murray, the Duke's fecond Son, to defcend to him at the Duke's Death, as if his elder Brother had been naturally dead. Lord James Murray was then in Parliament, as Mem- Journals. ber for the County of Perth; and he continued to fit till the Year 1724, when he fucceeded to the Title of Atholl, under the Act of Parliament. Though thus made the Heir-apparent of a Scots Title, and in Law, though not in Fact, the eldeft Son of a Scots Peer, the Refolution of 1708, and the fuppofed Rule of the Law of Scotland, recognized by that Refolution, were held not to reach his Cafe. 2d, Lord Strathnaver, eldeft Son of the Earl of Sutherland, died, leaving a Son, called likewife Lord Strathnaver, as Heir-apparent of his Grandfather. This Lord Strathnaver, under that Title, was elected Member of Par- Commons liament for the County of Sutherland, and fat unchallenged from 1727 Journals. to 1734, when he fucceeded his Grandfather in the Earldom. Thefe Inftances prove, that the Houfe of Commons hold the Refolution of 1708 to have been made, becaufe they were bound by the Letter of the Law of Scotland; but that they were not bound to go beyond the Letter. The Law of Scotland was fuppofed to exclude *the eldeft Son*, but had not exprefsly excluded *the Grandfon*, though immediate apparent Heir in the Dignity, or one whom an Act of Parliament fubftituted in the Place of the eldeft Son and Heir-apparent; though the Reafon of the Thing, and Spirit and Principle of the Law (if any Reafon or Principle can be

D   pointed

pointed out) muft go to the one Cafe as much as the other. If the
Objection of Ineligibility or Incapacity had been taken to Lord James
Murray, or to the younger Lord Strathnaver, it was forefeen that their
Anfwer would be, " As Commoners we are eligible, and capable by
" the general Law: Show us the Exception which applies in Terms
" to our particular Situation." The Plea was irrefiftible in the Britifh
Houfe of Commons ; and yet will any man believe that the Diftinction would have been liftened to by thofe who framed the Refolutions
of 1685 and 1689? So the eldeft Sons of Peers ought to have argued
in 1708, and may now argue, " As Commoners we are eligible and
" capable, under the clear, exprefs, comprehenfive Words of the Acts
" of 1587, 1661, and 1631, if we have in our Perfons the Qualifica-
" tion in Land, required by thofe Statutes. Show us the Law which
" excludes us, or the Provifo which excepts us. The only Difference
" between our Cafe and that of Lord James Murray and Lord Strath-
" naver, is, that the Words of the Refolutions of 1685 and 1689 were
" pointed againft eldeft Sons of Peers ; but the Doctrine of thefe Re-
" folutions, unfupported by any Statute, or by any Writer, and refuted
" by the Facts and the Statutes we appeal to, cannot be held for Law,
" or as Evidence of the Law."

Arguments and Authorities againft the Right of the Peers eldeft Sons confidered. IV. What has been faid or argued on the other Side of the Queftion
is next to be confidered. There is not, as already obferved, a Syllable
in the Statute Book, or a fingle Dictum in any Writer upon the Law
of Scotland, or Conftitution of Parliament, before the Union, which
gives Countenance to the Idea of the eldeft Sons of Peers being excluded. When Lord Stair and others lay down the general Rule,
That *all* the King's Freeholders are *obliged* (a Term for which modern
Ideas fubftitute *entitled*) to attend, and that the *Obligation* in the Cafe
of the Leffer Barons was permitted to be fulfilled by the Attendance of
Reprefentatives ; it feems ftrange, that no Notice whatever fhould be
taken of an Exception fo remarkable and (according to the Writers fince
the

the Union) ſo notorious. Either Lord Stair had never heard of the Reſolutions in 1685 and 1689, or, which is more probable, he thought them unworthy of the Notice of a ſyſtematical Writer.

Soon after the Union, two ſuperficial Treatiſes upon the Law of Elections for Scotland, were publiſhed, one by Mr. Forbes and the other by Mr. Spottiſwoode. The firſt ſtates, in ſo many Words, That the eldeſt Sons of Peers are ineligible; but the Reſolutions of 1685, 1689, and 1708, are his only Authorities. What Mr. Spottiſwoode ſays, will appear from what ſhall be immediately quoted from a ſubſequent Author, Mr. Wight, a Gentleman at the Scots Bar, who, within theſe few Years, has publiſhed a voluminous Work on the Conſtitution of the Parliament of Scotland, and the preſent Laws of Election. His great Experience in Election Queſtions, and indefatigable Induſtry, entitle one to conclude, that his Treatiſe contains the Subſtance of all the Arguments which have been, or which the beſt Lawyers imagined could be, urged againſt the Right of the Peers eldeſt Sons.

" The eldeſt Sons of Peers (ſays Mr. Wight), although infeſt in " Lands holden of the Crown, of the Extent and Valuation preſcribed " by Law, are incapable of electing, or of being elected, and therefore " cannot be admitted to the Roll. For this Spottiſwoode aſſigns the " following Reaſons: *That they are* QUASI *Peers of the Realm, and* " *have a Precedency allotted to them; that by their Birth they enjoyed* " *a Privilege to ſit in the Parliament of Scotland, and to hear the Tranſ-* " *actions in the Meetings of the Eſtates of the Kingdom, in order to fit* " *them for being worthy Members of that auguſt Aſſembly, when, upon* " *their Fathers' Death, they ſhould ſit in their Bench; and that, in* " *ancient Times, they were allowed to ſit and vote in Parliament as* " *Proxies for Peers.* But although, for a long Time before the Union, " the eldeſt Sons of Peers were not allowed to ſit in the Parliament of " Scotland as Repreſentatives either of Shires or of Boroughs, the " Records afford the moſt complete Evidence, that, in more ancient

Wight's Inquiry into the Riſe and Progreſs of Parliament. Edition in 4to. B. 3. C. 3. pp. 269, 270, 271.

" Times, and before the Reprefentation of Counties came to be thorough-
" ly eftablifhed, they fat in the fame Parliaments in which their Fathers
" attended as Peers. Inftances of this are to be found in the Parlia-
" ments 1478, 1481, and 1484; and in the Lift of the Parliament 1560,
" given in Keith's Hiftory, Page 146, we find William Mafter of Mari-
" fhall, John Mafter of Maxwell of Terriglis, Patrick Mafter of Linde-
" fay, Henry Mafter of Sinclair, and William Mafter of Glencairn.
" *Perhaps* they fat on thefe Occafions in virtue of their *happening to be*
" poffeffed of landed Property; and although we meet with no
" *explicit* Enactment of the Legiflature abolifhing this Practice, no
" Inftances of its being continued, after the laft mentioned Period, are to
" be found in the Records. It is alfo certain, that, for a *confiderable*
" *Time* before the Union, the eldeft Sons of Peers were *underftood to be*
" incapable of reprefenting either Counties or Boroughs; and as the
" Act 1707, Cap. 8. declared that none fhould be capable to elect
" or to be elected as Reprefentatives of Shires or Boroughs in Scotland,
" but thofe who were entitled to that Privilege by the Laws and Con-
" ftitution of Scotland, they were *thereby effectually debarred* from
" having any Voice in the Election of the 45 Commoners to be re-
" turned from that Part of the United Kingdom to the Britifh Par-
" liament; and a Declaration to that Effect was accordingly made by
" a Refolution of the Houfe of Commons in the Parliament of Great
" Britain, held in 1708."

It is worthy of Obfervation, that Mr. Wight, after laying down the
Propofition, That the eldeft Sons of Peers are incapable, refers to
Mr. Spottifwoode for the Reafons, without giving any Opinion as to
the Solidity of thofe Reafons, and plainly not wifhing to have it fuppofed that they met with his entire Approbation. What Mr. Spottifwoode has faid, and Mr. Wight has added, as from himfelf, in the
Paffage juft quoted, fhall be confidered in the Order in which the
feveral Particulars are there ftated.

I. *The*

1ft. *The eldeft Sons of Peers are quafi Peers of the Realm.* It is not eafy to annex an Idea to the Phrafe *quafi Peers,* which is certainly no technical Term, and it is believed occurs no where but in Mr. Spottifwoode. According to him, they were Peers, and no Peers. Peers without one effential Privilege of the Peerage ; in every Refpect, and in Law, upon a Level with the Commons, except having Titles, by Courtefy, and walking firft in a Proceffion. It is quite ludicrous to affign this as a Reafon for their being excluded from having Voices in Parliament.

2d. *They have a Precedency allotted to them.* It would be unneceffary to fay a Word on this, even if the eldeft Sons of Peers were the only Commoners who had Precedency allotted to them. But what does Mr. Spottifwoode fay to the Cafe of the younger Sons of Peers, and many others, who have Precedency ? What would the Man who could affign fuch a Reafon for the fuppofed Exclufion, have faid to the Cafes of Lord Strathnaver and Lord James Murray ?

3d. *By their Birth they enjoyed the Privilege of fitting in the Parliament to hear the Tranfactions.* If this were true, it could afford no Reafon for denying them an *efficient* Seat when poffeffed of a Qualification ; but there is no Authority for faying they had the Privilege by their Birth. They were admitted to be Auditors by the Favour of Parliament, juft as the Houfe of Lords, at this Day, permit the eldeft Sons of Peers and others to ftand behind the Throne. This appears by an Act or Refolution of Parliament in 1662, which it would be unneceffary to quote here, were it not of fome Confequence in another Part of the Argument, as it proves, That the eldeft Sons of Peers were not in the Language of Parliament called *Noblemen,* or meant to be defcribed by or comprehended in that Term when ufed. It declares that " None fhall be admitted to ftay in Parliament but the " ordinar Members of Parliament, viz. The Archbifhops, Bifhops, " *Noblemen,* Officers of State, Commiffioners from Shires and Burghs, " and the Clerk Regifter, Deputy, and Servants employed by him
" to

" to ferve in the Houfe; and, *befides thefe, Admittance is allowed to*
" *the eldeft Sons, and appearand Heirs male of Noblemen*, to the Senators
" of the College of Juftice, to the Knight Marifhall, &c.   And it is
" ordained, that none prefume to fit in the Benches, *fave the Nobility*
" *and Clergy*; that the Officers of State fit on the Steps of the Throne;
" that the Commiffioners of Shires and Burghs fit on the Forms
" appointed for them; *that Noblemen's eldeft Sons and Heirs aforefaid*,
" *fit on the lower Benches of the Throne*; that the Lords of Seffion fit
" at an Table which is to ftand betwixt the Throne and the Commif-
" fioners of Burghs."

Here the Terms *Noblemen* and *Nobility* are applied to thofe who are
themfelves Peers in the ftricteft Senfe, in exprefs diftinction from
their eldeft Sons.   Let this be compared with the Election-Law of
1661, referred to above.

4th. *In ancient Times they were allowed to fit and vote in Parliament*
as Proxies for Peers.   Of this Privilege, though it has been commonly
afferted, there is no Evidence whatever.   On the contrary, there is the
ftrongeft Prefumption that it never exifted.   The Acts of Parliament
1425 and 1503 appear to have allowed in early Times all Members
of Parliament to attend by Proxy; that of 1587, C. 34, to have put a
Stop to it; and that of 1617, to have allowed it again to Peers and
Prelates.   But no Conftruction of any of the Acts, or Commentary on
them, authorifes the Idea that the eldeft Sons enjoyed a Diftinction in
this Refpect.   The Rolls always mention when any Perfon attended
by Proxy, and fometimes give the Names of the Proxies of Peers.   In
feveral Inftances the Proxies were private Gentlemen, Commoners of
no Rank; *and not one Inftance is found of an eldeft Son being Proxy for*
his Father.   But even if it appeared that Peers eldeft Sons fome Times
fat as Proxies for their Fathers, it is evident that they frequently fat
in a more independent Capacity; for, in near Half the Inftances of
their being marked as attending, *their Fathers were alfo prefent.*

4   So

So much for Mr. Spottifwoode ; who, after this Difcuffion of his *Reafons*, will not probably be quoted, on the other Side, as an Authority. It is more probable, that the eldeft Sons of the Peers may refer to his Book, as proving how little the Subject was underftood in 1708, when a Scots Advocate, profeffing to write on the Law of Elections in 1710, difcovers fuch profound Ignorance of Hiftory and the Records . of Parliament.

After quoting Mr. Spottifwoode's Reafons in Support of the Rule, That Peers eldeft Sons are incapable, Mr. Wight's Acquaintance with the Records led him, and his Candour obliged him, to ftate Facts which prove that two Centuries ago, when all thofe *weighty* Reafons fubfifted in full Force, the Rule was unknown. He fays truly, " *That " there is the moft complete Evidence, that in more ancient Times, and before " the Reprefentation of Counties, the eldeft Sons of Peers fat in the fame " Parliaments in which their Fathers attended."* Confequently, they could not have been fitting as their Fathers' Proxies; and by *fitting*, Mr. Wight muft mean as conftituent Members, and not attending as Auditors only. He knew that this alfo was completely proved by the Records.

Inftances being given, Mr. Wight proceeds thus : " *Perhaps they " fat on thefe Occafions in virtue of their happening to be poffeffed of " landed Property."* Mr. Wight felt the neceffary Inference from the Facts he had ftated ; but it is evident that he confidered the Point as fettled by the Determinations of 1685, 1689, and 1708, and doubted of the Propriety of difturbing thofe Determinations. He knew that the Peers eldeft Sons muft have been entitled to fit when poffeffed of Property ; for nothing is more certain, than that the Parliament of Scotland was an Affembly of the Landholders, Tenants of the King ; and the legal conftitutional Idea was, not that they reprefented the People, or particular Orders of the People, but that they reprefented the Land.

The Introduction of Peers by Patent or Inveftiture, without Reference to Territory, and the admitting of certain Officers of the Crown to Seats in
Parliament,

Parliament, were Innovations of the Syſtem; but with theſe Exceptions, and at the Time when the Records prove that certain of the eldeſt Sons of Peers were Members, there is not the Shadow of Reaſon or Authority for imagining that any Perſon ſat, who had not in himſelf a Qualification in freehold Land, by virtue of which he was a Member, and by virtue of that alone. It cannot be too often repeated, that the Attendance was a feudal Obligation, and not a Privilege; an Obligation which none but thoſe liable to it, could be called on to fulfil, or could think of diſcharging. It is undeniable, that eldeſt Sons of Peers occaſionally attended : It is equally undeniable, that they attended as conſtituent and efficient Members, being elected of Committees. Nothing ſhort of abſolute Scepticiſm can therefore avoid the Concluſion, that the Peers Sons ſo entered on the Rolls as attending, ſat in their own Right as Freeholders, by virtue of their private Properties, in the ſame Way as if they had been in the broadeſt Senſe, Commoners, or Sons of Commoners.

Mr. Wight ſays, this was *before the Repreſentation of Counties came to be thoroughly eſtabliſhed*, meaning by the Act 1587; and he takes Notice of the negative Fact, of there being no Inſtance of a Peer's eldeſt Son ſitting after that Period. He admits at the ſame Time, that there is no *explicit* Enactment of the Legiſlature aboliſhing the former Practice : The Word *explicit* is here introduced, as the Word *perhaps* is in the firſt Part of the Sentence. If it was meant to inſinuate that there was ſome *unexplicit* Enactment, or ſome Act pointing that Way, Mr. Wight ſhould have referred to it. It has been already ſhown, that the Act 1587, and all the ſubſequent Statutes, ſo far from aboliſhing the Right, confirm it. If the Act 1587 made no other Alteration whatever upon the Conſtitution of Parliament, but that of excluding the perſonal Attendance of the Leſſer Barons or Freeholders (under the Degree of Prelates and Lords of Parliament), requiring *their* Attendance in Time to come by Repreſentatives choſen by all thoſe who before had a Title, or were obliged to attend in Perſon; and if the eldeſt Sons

of

of Peers were before that Act obliged to attend when poſſeſſed of Freeholds, and actually did attend, but were by the Act excluded as
Freeholders, in common with the general Maſs; it is impoſſible
to argue, that they were not after the Act, and under the pre-
ciſe Terms of it, entitled to elect and to be elected Repreſentatives of the Freeholders. If ſuch be the fair and obvious Conſtruc-
tion of the Act 1587, where is the ſubſequent Act which either expreſsly
or by Implication took away the Right?

No Inſtance can be produced of a Peer's eldeſt Son ſitting in the
Scots Parliament, by Election, after the Year 1587. But is it a
neceſſary Concluſion, that this aroſe from their being conſcious, or from its
being underſtood that they had no Right? It is otherwiſe and ſuffi-
ciently explained by the Principle ſo often alluded to; *the Obligation
to attend had ceaſed.* There was no Obligation to be elected a Repreſentative. Attendance had hitherto been conſidered as a Burden from
which the Vaſſals were glad to be relieved, of which the Act 1587
affords Evidence; for, according to it, his Majeſty, in diſpenſing
with the Attendance of the Leſſer Barons, was beſtowing a Favour, and he granted it upon Condition that the Freeholders obſerved
certain Promiſes they had made him; the Nature of which are now
unknown. In the ſame Light the being Repreſentative was conſidered for a long Period; the Repreſentative was entitled to his
Charges, and regularly demanded them.

There is not a groſſer, and yet not a more common Error, than
to eſtimate the Manners and Sentiments of a former Age by thoſe
of our own. To the People of the preſent Times, it ſeems a
natural and almoſt irreſiſtible Concluſion, from there being no
Inſtance of the eldeſt Sons of the Peers ſitting in Parliament, for
more than a Century, that they had no Right, or that if they ever had,
it muſt have been taken away; but when the Circumſtances are
conſidered, and the Views and Sentiments of the different Times are
compared, the Concluſion is altogether fallacious and erroneous. It

E   was

was no Object during the greater Part of the Period in Question for any Perfon to obtain a Seat in Parliament. It was then fhunned as much as it is now coveted ; and it was lefs an Object to the Sons of Peers than to other Gentlemen, becaufe their Confideration in the Country could receive little Addition by that Diftinction. It was not till towards the End of the 17th Century, that a Struggle for a Seat was heard of, and not till the very End of it, at the Period of the Revolution, that Contefts were carried on with Keennefs. The eldeft Sons of the Peers of Scotland then put in their Claim, but the Silence of a Century was interpreted againft them ; and a Rule of Exclufion, referring to no Law or Principle, was adopted to ferve the Purpofes of Party.

Another Way of accounting for the eldeft Sons of the Nobility appearing no longer in Parliament after the Alteration introduced by the Act 1587, is likewife fuggefted by the Manners of the Age. Thofe who hefitated not to take their Seats before, in Right of their Freeholds as Barons, and thereby on a Level with the Peers, difdained to come in by Election, to folicit Votes, and to reprefent a Body of Men whom they confidered as their Inferiors. The high Spirit or Pride of the Scots Nobility of thofe Times was exceffive ; and, in that Refpect, their eldeft Sons, according to Mr. Spottifwoode's Phrafe, were no doubt *quafi* Peers.

But whatever may have been their Reafon for defifting, if it was any other than that a legal Bar had been created, it cannot operate againft their Succeffors, if they can fhew inconteftably, that their Anceftors had the Right, and were in the Exercife of it.

Mr. Wight goes on to fay, *It is certain, that, for a confiderable Time before the Union, the eldeft Sons of Peers were underftood to be incapable of reprefenting either Counties or Boroughs.* A confiderable Time, is an Expreffion far from precife. Mr. Wight, however, can mean only a Period of little more than 20 Years ; for till Lord Tarbat dictated the Minute of 1685, there is not the leaft Authority for faying or fuppofing that the Idea had entered the Mind of any Man whatever. And if, by

I   its

its being *underflood*, is meant a *general* Underftanding, the whole of the
Propofition may be flatly denied. That there fhould have been a general
Underftanding on a Point of Law, and a Matter of Conftitutional Right
in its Nature moft remarkable, and yet that no Writer of the Period fhould
have taken the leaft Notice of it, is utterly incredible. In this Period,
Lord Stair, Lord Fountainhall, Sir George Mackenzie, and other emi-
nent Lawyers, compofed their Works. They treat of the Conftitution
of Parliament ; and Sir George Mackenzie mentions the Fact of Peers
eldeft Sons fitting in former Times as *Barons*, without hinting that the
Right had been abolifhed. Could fuch an Underftanding prevail, when
Mr. Higgins and his Counfel, in 1689, laying hold of every colourable
Objection to the Return of Lord Livingftone, forgot to ftate the fhort and
decifive one, that he was ineligible as the eldeft Son of a Peer ? If, by
the general Senfe of the Country, Peers eldeft Sons were by Law incapable of fitting in Parliament, would the Earl of Drumlanrig have been
allowed quietly to take his Seat as an Officer of State in 1693 ? Though
the Members *ex officio* certainly needed no Qualification, except their Offices, a legal Difability muft have operated againft them, as well as others.
But, above all, would the Debate, which has been mentioned, have occurred in the Union Parliament, if it had been underftood to be a fettled
Point, that the Peers Sons were ineligible ? Would the whole Body of
the Nobility, when ftruggling for the Right of their Sons, have preffed
for the Adoption of that Enactment, which declared, That none but thofe
who were by the Law, as it then ftood, capable of fitting in the Scots
Parliament, fhould reprefent Scotland in the Houfe of Commons of
Great Britain ?

Suppofing, for a Moment, that there was fuch a general Underftanding ; if founded in Error, can it make, or can it repeal Law ? Are Men
to be held incapable of fitting in Parliament, becaufe People took it into
their Heads that they were fo, in the Face of ancient Cuftom and pofi-
tive Statutes ? It is faid, that in Scotland an Act of Parliament may lofe
its Force and Operation by Defuetude ; and therefore, if the Capacity which

the

the eldeſt Sons of Peers once enjoyed had depended on any particular Statute, there might be Plauſibility, though not Solidity, in ſuch an Argument; becauſe it is evident, that the Neglect or Non-claimer of Individuals could not injure the legal Right of others not connected with them, and then unborn : But the eldeſt Sons of the Peers ſtand upon the common Law of the Land, which makes every Man eligible, unleſs he is diſqualified by poſitive Statute. They are claiming as Commoners, not as the eldeſt Sons of Peers; and in the former Character the Right has been all along exerciſed, and under it they muſt be entitled, unleſs they ſtand excluded by ſome Law pointed againſt Perſons of the latter Character in particular.

It is not the Right of the eldeſt Sons of the Peers alone which is to be conſidered; that of *the whole Body of the Electors in Scotland* is involved : Are they to be reſtrained in their Choice, by a Reſolution of one Branch of the Legiſlature, if that Reſolution is not founded in Law, and cannot be argued upon as *public* Law ? This Queſtion was ſo fully and ably diſcuſſed on a late memorable Occaſion, and, with Submiſſion, is ſo clear, that it ſeems unneceſſary to do more than hint its Connection with the preſent Subject.

Mr. Wight concludes, " That as the Act of 1707 declared, That " none ſhould be capable to elect, or be elected, Repreſentatives of " Shires or Boroughs in Scotland, but thoſe who are entitled to this " Privilege by the Laws and Conſtitution of Scotland, the eldeſt Sons " of Peers were thereby effectually debarred from having any Voice " in the Election of the forty-five Commoners to be returned from " that Part of the United Kingdom to the Britiſh Parliament." Upon this it is enough to obſerve, that it is a mere begging of the Queſtion. The eldeſt Sons of the Peers maintain, that they were entitled to the Privilege at the Time of paſſing the Act of 1707 ; and therefore are not debarred by it from electing, or being elected, Repreſentatives for Scotland in the Houſe of Commons of Great Britain.

Having thus met every Part of Mr. Wight's Argument, it may be right to take Notice of a few words on this Subject, which occur in the

the Works of another Author, and a moſt reſpectable one, Lord Bankton, who publiſhed his Inſtitutes in 1752.   His Lordſhip ſays,
" The eldeſt Sons of Peers cannot repreſent Shires or Boroughs in
" Scotland; *Becauſe they muſt have their full Repreſentation, without*
" *Encroachment from the Eſtate of Peers.*"   B. 4. Tit. 1. § 41.   He
quotes no Authority for the Poſition ; and the Reaſon he gives, ſhows
how difficult it is to figure the Colour of a Reaſon.   The Deciſion of
1708 had impreſſed on People's Minds, that ſuch was the Law ; and
from Spottiſwoode downwards, every Writer, ſuppoſing there muſt be a
Reaſon, gives that which firſt occurs to himſelf.   Here Lord Bankton
ſuppoſes that Peers eldeſt Sons are *of the Eſtate of Peers.*   What Ground
there can be, for ſaying People are of an Eſtate, who do not enjoy a
ſingle Privilege of that Eſtate, may be ſubmitted to the common Senſe
of every Perſon.

The Acts of Parliament which have been referred to, relate only to
the Elections for Counties ; and it may be obſerved, perhaps, that
nothing has been ſaid on the Right of repreſenting the Boroughs in
Scotland; but it is unneceſſary, becauſe it will be admitted, that if the
eldeſt Sons of the Peers are entitled to be elected for the Counties, they
muſt be capable to repreſent the Boroughs likewiſe.   It was common,
down to the Time of the Union, for thoſe who belonged properly to
the Eſtate of Barons, to be elected Commiſſioners for Boroughs; and
an Attempt in the laſt Century to check the Practice, proved abortive.
In a Word, it is now eſtabliſhed, that no Qualification is neceſſary, to be
elected for Scots Boroughs, and every Britiſh Subject, under the Degree of a Peer, is eligible, unleſs excluded by ſome poſitive Act of the
Legiſlature, on account of perſonal Situation.

UPON THE WHOLE MATTER,

As it is undeniable, that the eldeſt Sons of the Peers ſat in Parliament
before the Year 1587, as Commoners or Leſſer Barons, in their own
Right, when poſſeſſed of Freeholds :

As

As the only Alteration in the Conftitution, fince that Period, is that the Leffer Barons fit by their Reprefentatives, inftead of attending perfonally or individually:

As the Intention of the Act 1587, was to beftow the Right of electing, or being elected, Reprefentatives, upon all the Leffer Barons fo difcharged from perfonal Attendance:

As by the unequivocal Terms of that, and all the fubfequent Election Statutes, the Right is vefted in *all Freeholders* under the Degree of Prelates and Lords of Parliament, poffeffed of Land to a certain Extent, and there is not a Word in any of the Acts excepting Peers eldeft Sons, being Freeholders, either directly, or by any Implication:

As the Determinations of the Scots Parliament in 1685 and 1689, had no Foundation in the Law or Conftitution of Scotland, and are accounted for from the Circumftances and Spirit of the Times:

As the Determination of the Britifh Houfe of Commons in 1708, appears to have been founded fingly on the Scots Precedents; and there is every Reafon to think that the Matter was not properly explained upon, that Occafion:

And as the Right of electing, or of being elected, if vefted by Law, cannot be loft by difufe:

> It is to be expected, from the Juftice, Liberality, and good Senfe of the proper Judicature, That, upon a Reconfideration of the Queftion, and of the Evidence here alluded to, or other fatisfactory Evidence to be laid before them, the Principle of the Refolution in 1708, as erroneous, will be REVERSED; and that the eldeft Sons of the Peers of Scotland will be declared entitled by Law to fit as Reprefentatives of the Commons of Scotland in Parliament.

APPENDIX, N° I.

Copy of the Roll of Parliament 1481.

XIII Aprilis in dicto Parliamento p̄ntibus Wīllmo Archiepiſcopo Sancti Andree, Johanne ēpiſcopo Glaſguen, Jacobo epiſcopo Dunkelden, Roberto epiſcopo Aberdonenſ; Abbatibus de Kelſow, Corſraigwell, Halywood, Priore de Inchmaquholme, ... Domino Cancellario, Comitibus de Anguſiic, Ergile, Athole, Buchane, Monteith, Merſchell, et Rothes; Dominis de Dernlie, *Erſkin*, Oliphant, Glammys, Cathkert, Gray, Cariile, Lyle, Kennedy; prepoſito de Linclowden, Secretario, Clerico regiſtri, prepoſito Sancti Andree; Officiale Laudonie; Magiſtro Alexᵣᵒ Murray, Magiſtro Georgio de Carmychell, Rectore de Flyſk; preceptore de Torfychin; Roberto Crechtown de Sanquhare *Magro de Erſkin*, David Lindiſſay milite, Domino de Dalwolſy, Dno de Bas, Domino Jacobo Liddale milite, *Magro de Halys*, Dno de Corſtorphin, Jacobo Crechton de . . . . , Johanne de Haldane, Johanne Murray de Tuchadam, Arthuro Forbes, Gilberto Johneſtoune, Dno de Torry, Waltero Stewart, Johane Ross de Montgrenane, Dno Jacobo Crechtoune de Carnys; *Magro* Ricardo Lawſone; David Rollock Commiſſario de Dundee, Archebaldo Manderſtoun Commiſſario de Berwick, Bertholomeo Carnys, Alexᵣᵒ Turing, et Alexᵉ Bonkill Commiſſariis de Edinburgh, Johane Hadingtoune Commiſſario de Perth, ... Commiſſario de North Berwick.

APPENDIX, N° II.

Copy of the Roll of Parliament 1478.

PARLIAMENTUM excellentiſſimi principis, & d̄n̄ī n̄r̄ī d̄n̄ī Jacobi terti dei gra Scotorum regis illuſtrᵐⁱ tent. & inchoat apud Edinburghi primo die menſis Martii anno dni 1478 Sēctis vocatis et curia Affirmat Abſen patent ad extra

Comparuerunt

Epi
Glaſguen
Dunkelden
Aberdonen
Moravien
Brechinen
Dumblanon
Ergadien
Orkaden

Abbtes	Co͞ites et barones
Prior Stiandri	Comes de Marr
Abbas de cales	Comes Atholie
Abbas de Abberbrothok	Comes Anguſie
Abbas ſanc̄te crucis	Comes Craufurdie
Abbas de Melroſs	Comes Buchanie
Abbas de Scond	Comes de Ergile
Abbas de Kilwynning	Comes de Menteth
Abbas de Lundoris	Comes de Mortoun
Abbas de Newbotle	Comes de Rothes
Abbas de Inchechaffʳ	Comes de Eroule Conaſtabᵘˢ Sco.
Abbas de columbe	Comes Merſchiale Marˡᵘˢ Sco.

Abbas

Abbas de Jedworth
Abbas de Corſagwell
Abbas de Culroſs
Abbas de Dundranane
Abbas de Paſleto

Dn̄i Parliati	Burgorum Commiſſaȓii
Dns Avandale cancellaȓius	Berwick
Dns de Erſkyn	Jedwort
Dns Deraly	Selkirk
Dns Haliburtoun	Peblis
Dns Maxwell	Lanark
Dns Sommervile ·	Dumfres
Dns Lindeſay de Byris	Wigtoun
Dns Kennedy	Kirkudbry'
Dns Kilmawaris	Aire
Dns Flemyng	Irwin
Dns Crechtoun	Dumbretain
Dns Borthwick	Strivelyne
Dns Glammis	Linlithgw
Dns Graye	Edinburgh
Dns Seytoune	Hadingtoun
Dns Oliphant	North berwic
Dns Caithkert	Dunbar
Dns Lyle	Kingorne
Dns de Innermeth	Innerkethin
Dns Carlile	Caraile
Dns Hume	Couper
	Saintandros
	Perth
	Forfare
Barones	Dunde
Preceptor de Torſichen	Brechin
Dns de Yeſter	Monthroſs
Dns de Baſs	Abirdene
Magr de Halis	
Magr de Erſkyn	
Dns de Pettruſy	
Dns de Caldor	
Dns de Ochiltre	
Willmꝰ Edmondſtoun de Duntreth	

F

Dns

Dns de Auchinlek
Dns de Halkete
Dns de Dalwoulfy
Dns de Haltoun
Dns de Cragy Walace
Dns de Lufe
Dns de Stobhall
Dns de Tulibardin
Dns de Elliotiftoun
Dns de Halkeriftoun liddale
Dns de Leftalrig

N. B. Under the Title *Barenes* none of the Nobility are included. *Dominus* de Yefter, is the *Laird* of Yefter, or Owner of the Lands of Yefter. There was no fuch Title of Nobility as Yefter at this Period. There never was fuch a Title of Nobility as *Bafs*. And thus the *Maſters* of Hales and Erſkin, eldeft Sons of the Lords Hales and Erſkin, are here claſſed as *Leſſer* Barons, after the Lairds of Yefter and Bafs.

The Original of this Roll, and many others, is in Columns, and blank Spaces left, as here reprefented.

www.ingramcontent.com/pod-product-compliance
Lightning Source LLC
Chambersburg PA
CBHW021445090426
42739CB00009B/1647